OPC2024A

Black Eyes Publishing UK & Gloucestershire Poetry Society
Open Poetry Competition 2024 Anthology

OPC2024A

Black Eyes Publishing UK & Gloucestershire Poetry Society
Open Poetry Competition 2024 Anthology

Black Eyes Publishing UK

OPC2024A
© Gloucestershire Poetry Society 2024

Published 2024
Black Eyes Publishing UK
Gloucester GL1 3ET (UK)

www.blackeyespublishinguk.co.uk

ISBN: 978-1-913195=34-2

All poems in this anthology remain within the copyright of the individual poets. They have asserted their moral right under the Copyright, Designs and Patents Act, 1988, to be identified as the authors of their work.

All Rights reserved. No part of this publication may be reproduced, copied, stored in a retrieval system, or transmitted, in any form or by any means, without the prior written consent of the copyright holder(s), nor be otherwise circulated in any form of binding or cover other than that in which it is published and without a similar condition being imposed on the subsequent purchaser.

A CIP catalogue record for this title is available from the British Library.

Editor: Peter Lay

www.thegloucestershirepoetrysociety.com

Cover design: Jason Conway, The Daydream Academy.
www.thedaydreamacademy.com

Introduction

It gives me great pleasure to introduce this anthology *OPC2024A* of poems from **The Black Eyes, Gloucestershire Poetry Society (GPS) 2024 Open Poetry Competition**. The total entry for the 2024 competition was 713 poems, with all entries being considered anonymously, throughout the process.

Longlisting was undertaken by Josephine Lay (Former Dir. Of Ops for the GPS & lead editor for Black Eyes Publishing) with assistance from Jason Conway (Current Dir. Of Ops for the GPS). The Longlist consisted of 69 poems. All longlisted poems were eligible for this anthology. However, several eligible poems, were withdrawn, once the results had been announced, to be either submitted elsewhere, or re-worked.

The Longlist was judged by Helen Ivory (her judges report is included in this anthology) Helen produced a Shortlist of 10 poems, before settling on the final results.

The GPS Friendship Prize was judged by Josephine, from the 55 poems submitted to **The Black Eyes, Gloucestershire Poetry Society (GPS) 2023 Open Poetry Competition,** by GPS Friendship Members. Josephine's judges report is included in this anthology, together with the poems included in the results.

Finally, many thanks, and congratulations on their choices to the judges.

Peter Lay
Black Eyes Publication UK
December 2024

Contents

9	Black Eyes/GPS 2023 Open Poetry Competition Judges Report: Helen Ivory
11	GPS Friendship Prize Judges Report: Josephine Lay
13	20 Ways to Skin a Spell - Sujatha Menon
14	Advent 2023 – Tudor Griffiths
15	A ghazal for the stranger and his children - Leah Okenwa Emegwa
17	A Saturday Morning Waking up in York - Rosie Aziz
18	Alice's Endgame - Pamela Job
19	Analogue - Stephen Littlejohn
21	Aubade - Ian Parker Dodd
22	Bach contemplates the playing of his Cello Suite No 5 after the Bombing, Kharkiv - Tess Biddington
24	Bathing - Michael Farry
25	Beyond - Julia Deakin
26	Blue Lips Don't - Kate Fenwick
27	Case Notes - David Hale
28	Collective Callings - Clare Morris
30	Confessions of a Werewolf - Iain McClure
31	counter-manifesto - Junxin Tang
33	Crones of the Underworld - Sujatha Menon
35	Crystal - Iris Anne Lewis
36	Dark Matter - Charlotte Faulconbridge
38	Death of a Pheasant - Julian Wakeling
39	Donna and Child - Geoff Yorath
40	Elevations - Julie Allan
41	Entanglement - Gwyneth Box
42	Every-day office - Kathryn Southworth
43	FLORENCE - Francesca La Nave
44	Haven't you already said all there is to say about rape - Katrina Moinet
45	Hinterland - Julie Allan
46	Hunger - Maggie Mackay
47	Jungle Epitaph - Adam Ali-Hassan
49	KASHUBABEL - Anna Blasiak
50	L'Inconnue de la Seine - Penny Howarth
51	Metamorphosis - Charlie Markwick

52	**Mistle Thrush** - Carol Sheppard
53	**Nail Therapy** - Alison
54	**Night Fauna** - Helen Butlin
56	**Our golden record** - Deborah Finding
57	**Poetry Nights** - Val Ormrod
58	**Protest Song** - Sophia Argyris
60	**Sarah Polgrains Song of the Wind** - Jane Burn
62	**State of Mind** - Nigel Kent
64	**STRIPTEASE** - Marilyn Timms
66	**Tell Me** - Geoff Yorath
67	**That's Entertainment** - Oz Hardwick
68	**The Cord** - Graeme Ryan
70	**The fox withstanding** - Catherine Wilson Garry
72	**The Grandmother Hypothesis** - Rhian Thomas
73	**the place of turtles** - Milla van der Have
75	**The Seed Cleaner's Inventory** - Sujatha Menon
77	**The Toddler of Sardasht's Tale -** Sandra Mary Chambers
79	**The vacillations of the scholar Wu Mi (吴宓) 1894-1978**
	- Helen Wing
80	**Touch** - Diana Sanders
81	**We're Off Bloody Boating** - Rosie Barrett
82	**What a piece of work** - Marcus Tickner
83	**You Made Me a Corn Dolly** - Sue Finch
84	**Your robot girlfriend** - Deborah Finding

Helen Ivory: Judge's Report
Black Eyes / Gloucestershire Poetry Society 2024 Open Poetry Competition

When judging a poetry competition, you are compelled to ask yourself questions –
the biggest of these: *What is Poetry?* And then looking at each of the poems *Is this it?* Still further questions as you're arranging a smaller and smaller pile of poems into a fan shape on the floor – *Does this poem invite a second reading?* And when you put the poem down after several readings in which it has continued to unpack itself in your head and go into another room and start to do something altogether different – *Does the poem call to you? Has it secreted parts of itself inside your head, in your heart?* The further along the enquiry goes, the more subjective the search becomes.

Two of my favourite quotes about poetry are from Donald Hall who writes that a poem is: "human inside talking to human inside." And then there is Charles Simic who says something so utterly Charles Simic: "Poetry: three mismatched shoes at the entrance of a dark alley." These quotes express something about what I personally look for in a poem. There should be a human connection – I need to *feel* the poem as well as engage with it intellectually. The *feeling* part of a poem might be difficult to articulate, but it's the element that will for me, warrant the poem further readings.

So, upon further investigations I am looking closely at those mismatched shoes, the mystery of them. Just what is down that dark alley? It's not so much solving a puzzle – because a puzzle has particular ends - it's more to do with working out what it's doing and why a poem might have a certain effect on you. Sometimes you never know exactly what it is and sometimes it can be a mutable thing, depending on where you are in your life. I've learnt to be ok with that. There is something to be said for not picking apart a living thing in order to interrogate what gives it life.

These particular poems connected with me in the selection process and refused leave my head.

In first place **20 Ways to Skin a Spell.** I am drawn to spells, I have written them myself, so was a little wary of being seduced by this poem for simply that reason. I walked away from it a few times, but it kept tapping me on the shoulder – surprise! This poem is a manifestation of serious play. I enjoyed the experimental nature of its mechanism and also its layout which feels a completely logical, backwards ghosting of each line. It reads like a performance and I hear those between-lines played shakily on an old-fashioned wax record, spun widdershins. I love the richly charged language and how the poem uses both science and spell making practices in its recipe for disarming a virus.

In second place *The fox withstanding* centres on another subject I know a lot about – domestic abuse. Akin to the first placed poem, I stood back from this for a bit because it speaks directly to me, and I was wary of it. But it called to me again and again and wouldn't let me go. The extended metaphor unmakes itself halfway through as the fox as spirit guide speaks up, so the narrator can look you square in the eye and state exactly what fear can do. This poem is 'human inside talking to human inside', and it spoke directly to me.

In third place *Sarah Polgrain's Song of the Wind* is a rich and wonderful narrative poem, based on a dark true story/ folk story. I loved the language of this poem, the Cornish dialect – it's a joy to read out loud.

Highly Commended:

Mistle Thrush is written in the voice of a mistle thrush which has heard a lot about itself in folklore and such. The poem shows how creatures carry so much human fear and imagination on their shoulders when transmuted to symbol and story.

First: 20 Ways to Skin a Spell - Sujatha Menon
Second: The fox withstanding - Catherine Wilson Garry
Third: Sarah Polgrain's Song of the Wind - Jane Burn

Highly Commended: Mistle Thrush - Carol Sheppard

Josephine Lay: Judge's Report
Black Eyes / Gloucestershire Poetry Society 2024 Open Poetry Competition
GPS Friendship Prize

This year, 2024, there were an increased number of entries to the GPS Open Poetry Competition, which made the job of longlisting more challenging. Friendship Group entries, however, were slightly down, maybe because we brought the date of the competition forward a month, I don't know.

One friendship member has a special mention in the overall competition for the poem, 'Mistle Thrush', so congratulations to that poet. For me, there wasn't a particular single poem that stood out as an obvious winner. There were in fact five poems that caught my attention and remained with me so that I had to return to them all and reread them many times. Because of that I found it hard to choose just one winner. Therefore, this year the prize will be split between two very different poems.

Several facets of the poem *Crystal* glinted at me, in its pared back style. An example of good editing, where less is more. The sharp contrast of the start of the poem to its dark ending, had me re reading it over and over. The second poem that caught me emotionally was *The Grandmother Hypothesis*. May be because I am a grandmother, I related to its message. This quite short poem packs so much into a few lines; the desiccation expected in old age, tears shed with the pain of watching children suffer unnecessarily, and finally the thought that other life forms have a deeper understanding of unity than we do. Other poems that commended themselves to me were: *Elevations* – I loved learning what only the stonemason sees. *Advent 2023* – a powerful way of portraying war in the Middle East. *You Made me a Corn Dolly* – a tight and poignant poem.

The GPS Friendship Prize jointly goes to:
Crystal – Iris Anne Lewis
The Grandmother Hypothesis – Rhian Thomas

Highly Commended:
Elevations – Julie Allan
Advent 2023 – Tudor Griffiths
You Made Me a Corn Dolly – Sue Finch

Longlisted, Shortlisted, 'Winner'
Black Eyes/GPS 2024 Open Poetry Competition

Sujatha Menon

The capsid or protein shell of many viruses have an icosahedral structure composed of 20 equilateral triangles fused together in a spherical form. This is the most stable and optimal shape for enclosing genetic material.

20 Ways to Skin a Spell

Frack the egg, make 3 holes: Maiden   Mother   Crone   then blow   until you are hollow

Bleed each yolk   with the hexagonal oath   of an Allen key cussing

Splice the whites   meringued   sweet tongue of Yarrow, Mugwort & Holy Basil

Now reconstitute in non-metallic ratio : minus any numbers that may multiply with wings

Remove the pips   wear what's left like leather   or dream creamily in fur

Deactivate the shell   let it lie like a mouse sleeping in a beast waiting to shrivel

Flatten   with a moon-head hammer   chisel charms in its flagrant walls

Pin it to the heart gone wild   oh shining trophy of vowels!   but let it still be animal

Stroke it to death   *Sing* it to sleep   backwards

'Highly Commended'
The GPS Friendship Prize

Tudor Griffiths

Advent 2023

The dawn from on high shall break upon us
with starburst white hot shrapnel.
Maryam sits weeping with Rachel in
tunnels where vengeance is wreaked and conceived.

Gabriel is coming through still rubbled streets.
His purpose is clear, while other eyes flit
fearfully searching for bread or a tin
of boiled chicken or surplus sardines.

Lo-Ammi deep rumbles secure in his tank,
phosphorus-tipped shells at command of AI,
the drone-driven destroyer.
Salvation comes to him, not from him.

While Maryam weeps,
one side of her Gospel, the other Jihad
and the child within her
will be born.

Longlisted
Black Eyes/GPS 2024 Open Poetry Competition

Leah Okenwa Emegwa

A ghazal for the Stranger and his children

Land of lakes and tranquil archipelagos welcomes the Stranger and his children.
All that pursued are now distant, in this safe haven for the children.

Except for two months in a year, the sun is weak, hides or shines but no warmth.
The sun is not the sun without its warmth, says the Stranger to his children.

Dreamer turned cleaner, Stranger seeking greener pasture.
His unsatisfied personal longings, a sacrifice for the future of the children.

You are strange, the Stranger is told every time he speaks or does his customs.
Learn our customs and you will be fine, you and your children.

More strange things, the Stranger discovers day by day.
Life in a new land is life in a layered maze. Lost, he is losing some of his children.

Oh, the children! Foreigners at school, foreigners at home
An in-between identity in the land of lakes. That's their lot, the Stranger's children.

Wolves in sheep clothing lie in wait, seeking all children feeling "in-between."
"Come," they say, "let us play", fierceness hidden from the children.

With the feeling of "in-between" comes a deep longing to fit in and be accepted.
Wolves or ourselves, who will evoke acceptance and identity in the children?

Hurry, hurry, Wolves are winning! Crime, death and mental health nightmares hover.
The Stranger's safe haven, now a scary land for the children.

More Police, decision makers say. "Dark" bulb moment I dare say!
O sun, you are the sun, warm or not, rise and shine for the children.

Oh Leah, stand by the Stranger and scream with him: We are not strange.
Your maze feels strange! Give us tools, show some patience, and watch us guide the children.

Sun, moon, and stars of the land of lakes, shine, shine for the children.
Land of lakes and tranquil archipelagos, arise, arise, for the children.

Longlisted
Black Eyes/GPS 2024 Open Poetry Competition

Rosie Aziz

A Saturday Morning Waking up in York.

The dawn drags, twisted in stuffy linen,
but never stirring
or living. You're used to the drip

of the alarm clock on the windowsill,
and every click is a fraction
slower than your pulse, but you don't

dwell. After all, the potted succulent ,
an unwilling gift
is now hunched on the ledge, leaves

mushed into the soil and gravel,
and somewhere beyond
the pane, a gaggle of geese hiss

water between their teeth and tongues,
screaming blasphemy,
each possessive shriek cracking

into your windowpanes, ricocheting down
leaf-sodden drainpipes
and sliding into gutters like an echo

lost in its tracks. The sound prickles
in your fingertips with a silent
bellow.

A silence that flattens the skyline
of your bedroom,
embroiders your skin. Each thread twines

into your linen, twisting knots
where your fingers still fist
the rumble of night beneath the covers.

Longlisted, Shortlisted
Black Eyes/GPS 2024 Open Poetry Competition

Pamela Job

Alice's Endgame

After a quarrel with time, she says
I think we should change lobsters and retire.

Hold on to the chair back my dear.
She generally gives herself very good advice.

Now she spends hours by the Pool of Tears
where she hears more than twice as many songs

sung about snails and whiting than she thought
she ever knew in the first plaice.

She can't remember spellings, the word
'quadrille': she doesn't think it's edible . . .

I can't explain myself - I'm not myself, you see.
All this vocal mobbing, there's been so much change.

Polyphonic sounds repeat themselves
until she can't tell unicorns from trees.

Or walruses from carpenters - she sounds very old
indeed, but she knows she can't go back to yesterday

because she'd never find herself. She realises too late
this is the consequence of giving away her childhood.

Longlisted
Black Eyes/GPS 2024 Open Poetry Competition

Stephen Littlejohn

Analogue

It's a question of balls. His are unabridged, ample
like valves. He survived the olden days,
favoured leaves of hemp in his pipe to the grape,
the lash and a hard word to the cross;
he was at Gomorrah.

These days of course it's all about the tech:
smoke and lasers; targets pinned to the monochrome
by drones with night vision
but the ends are always the same. It still takes balls
to bring a human being down. Analogue

squats in the backs of men's minds,
waiting for a signal.
He sifts through thoughts like waves on a beach
splashing in the saturation layers
where long days decompose

into sleep's shallows,
looking for the spark that will set the sea on fire.
Sometimes he finds himself inside your dreams, dressed
for a night of bad behaviour,
tumescent in his thong, the muscles

of his thighs and abdomen hardened seams,
shale among flesh-toned fireclay
and you'll follow him up some neon-lit stretch
lined with sinister teahouses,
interiors laid out in gritty little vignettes:

Judith in her beam of light, slicing
through tendon and bits of throat;
Christ as a dead man, held by hands
that could have fixed a broken clutch,
His wound fingered like a snatch.

About to walk away you'll waken, belligerent,
but Analogue will still be there, embedded,
a subtle outline in the sun-struck curtains.
Gazing at it, you'll drift, dissipate and
in the slushy equilibrium he'll become you.

Longlisted
Black Eyes/GPS 2024 Open Poetry Competition

Ian Parker Dodd

Aubade

Breathless silence, the banshee keening
startled me awake. It was over.
Too tired to cry. Everything was still.
Your skin white porcelain. Day was dawning.

Sunbeams flicker on the red waste bin,
the dark blue towel — the last
of your long practice in practicalities
for catching blooms of blood.

There's nothing to be disturbed about.
You had long since grieved your song,
your intellect, your love response.

Now it's ordinary again, the washing up
eating breakfast, phone calls to make.
I watch a vixen trot through the garden

Longlisted
Black Eyes/GPS 2024 Open Poetry Competition

Tess Biddington

Bach contemplates the playing of his Cello Suite No 5 after the Bombing, Kharkiv

What if I were that genius?
It means nothing apart from the freedom
granted by those who believe
my Prince
who appoints me Kappelmeister
and under that disguise to stray
into the secular

Only the music

Anna dear wife
do not blot the score
Curtsey, curtsey before
the Prince but do not blot
do not slur the score
unless I say

precisely where

Anna, they will speculate
that you are me
poor subjugated female
poor ink-stained fingertips
devoted to notation

but your voice ah your voice

It has a melancholy tongue this instrument
I have determined it should speak alone
And for itself
whatever chamber attempts to contain it

This sky I remember over Leipzig

mid-winter
extracting my soul into that blue
emptiness between each note
Listen   listen   the silences are

We stray so much from the source
Nothing of this is lively
February-chilled cellist alone in his nest of rubble
coaxing lament with the bow
Iskanders having written their own scores
each note a blackened aperture
in this stately façade

Is this my legacy to be played
in the shambles of war? I give hope
from here?

Longlisted
Black Eyes/GPS 2024 Open Poetry Competition

Michael Farry

Bathing

She marched us down the sunken lane
between funereal oaks
past a cousin's dark farmhouse
its dog worrying at the gate
to sunlight on the shore where she stripped and bathed us.

It was all strange to us, inlanders
the expanse of light, the warmth
of worn stone, sharp grass below
and the timid lapse of waves
the country opposite close but inaccessible.

I recalled his September stories,
how out there death rode the waves
and wondered if some locals
heard from here the clinging screams
then fled, helpless, as the men went silent, one by one.

They should have stayed, she said, caught
the Ballina bus, arrived
late at Farniharpy fair
cancelling that dire month
washed-up bodies, inquests and unhappy survivors.

Even then no-one learned to swim
and it's far too late for me
still unwilling to roll my
trousers up at the seaside
pretend to have fun in a foot of salt sea water.

Why this disturbs me now I can't tell.
Is it because a rain storm
is pelting down outside
hammering on my window
the water pooling in each innocent reflection?

Longlisted
Black Eyes/GPS 2024 Open Poetry Competition

Julia Deakin

Beyond

the 'bloodbath' call to arms,
beyond Boko Haram's child kidnappings
the cloth-offed teens
and black-skin-blanking facial recognition schemes

beyond the millions blown to bits
by deep fake rhetoric, some species surely
will slip through: some crow
fly out of range, some rodent gorge

and flourish, some ewe retrieve
her live lamb from the pyre.
Some sonar-signalling cetaceans, echolocating bats,
chemically-networked ants,

some cactus dormouse singing rodent wisdom
to her young, and some – some human will re-set
a neural network to decode what 'dumb' creatures
have been saying all along. What they think.

Longlisted
Black Eyes/GPS 2024 Open Poetry Competition

Kate Fenwick

Blue Lips Don't

Seduced by absolute zero's Judas kiss,
your fingers, arctic, reached for the morgue.
At the amber light our dirty emergency
thawed onto the ambulance floor
pooling an accumulation of silence.

Cryovolcanoes erupt on Saturn's
two moons, spew frigid tears.
Unique but fallen
we are written in rain, not ice.

When your breath bites back
and the fissure at your feet tempts
you to crystallize, loosen your straps
step into liquidity.

We aren't designed to be frozen
death is a forecast not a choice.
Fail into me, I can warm you–
I've learnt there's nothing colder
than a blade on a wrist in hot water.

Longlisted
Black Eyes/GPS 2024 Open Poetry Competition

David Hale

Case Notes

Minutes after her arrival
she was causing mayhem and words didn't calm her.
Do normal, the therapist said,
do something to help yourself,
so I imagined her as a box bound by chains
to which the key was lost.
But that didn't work.
So I saw her as a butterfly
scorched by the sun, but she threw a knife
through the kitchen window,
my dreams filled up with wings and broken glass.
So I visualised her as a stray
cornered in the crypt of a derelict church.
But that didn't work either.
Hours I spent, trying to see beyond
the exterior to the shape within.
Until one morning down by the cove
I pictured her as a jellyfish trailing a bloom of toxic cords
and stinging anything in her way
From that moment, I knew there was hope.

Longlisted
Black Eyes/GPS 2024 Open Poetry Competition

Clare Morris

Collective Callings

And what of those who duck and dive, bobbing in their best bib and tucker or *chak-chak-chak-chak* with glint in their eyes, cacklesome confederates who've always been wise to the black and the white of that trick with mirrors? Let's call them a mischief, yes, a mischief of magpies; I like that.

And what of those who perch, prim potentates among plum trees, or dine dappletime-drowsy beneath thistles and teasels, as they trill the full-throated thrum of each midmorning's magic, *teLLIT-teLLIT-teLLIT*? Let's call them a charm, yes, a charm of goldfinches; I like that.

And what of those, the solitary ones, bowed brittle with winter's brunt and buffet, seared sharp with summer's withering; does any collective compassion shield them? Hear each one creak and groan as she rustles up a refuge for those small, sleeping things that gather in the folds of her dress, frayed now with wear, no time to mend, her arms stretched wide across her little world - above the hazel dormice dozing in brambles; above the cirl buntings as they *zizizi zizi* before they *hush hush hush* to dream in bushy beds of green; as her supple spine defines flyways for greater horseshoe bats so they can forage without fear; as her limbs, lichen-lit with rare radiance, offer rot holes ripe for nuthatch nests: as her blackthorn shoots show where brown hairstreaks can commit their eggs to her care; as she captures particulates; as she increases infiltration; as she slows water flows -

And in this act of purifying love, look now, there, just there - see how the land thrives, is reborn again in a glorious groundswell of rejoicing, a resurging of earth's worth –

But look again, there, just there - see how her hands are broken again and again by flail and cutter bar and chain saw, too frequent, too thoughtless in their visiting, as she stands sole bearer of her suffering.

Do you hear her voice borne on the breeze?

Not yet, not yet; wait for the third year at least, so that we might all mend and in mending, wend wise ways to make amends for all our days ...

So summon her scattered tribe, her shattered clan, her splintered kin. Stitch them, patch them, help them whole. Call each by name: the blackthorn, the elder, the hazel, the ash, the oak, the holly, the yew - these few but so, so many more, their songs echoing long through the centuries. And then, let's call them a healing, yes, a healing of hedgerows; I like that.

And so let the healing begin...

Longlisted
Black Eyes/GPS 2024 Open Poetry Competition

Iain McClure

Confessions of a Werewolf

Yellowed as old horse teeth
the full moon rose, cursing me,
one cloudless solstice night
when I was just seventeen
and fell upon all fours.
Nails dropped from their bloody beds,
replaced by curling claws,
vertebrae stretched long and low,
virgin skin became a pelt
as soft and dark as shadow.
I lifted up my snout to bay
and my howl was answered.

We ran through the winter
in forests with no paths,
printing snow with footfalls,
sleeping where leaves drifted,
tasting blood upon our tongues,
mating in the final frosts
with fire in our muscles
like venom in the blood,
speaking with all the birds
as God speaks with his angels.

That was long ago. Now
my wife sleeps beside me,
our firstborn in the cradle,
the cat close by the cooling fire.
Each dawn I shave my face,
go to work in polished shoes -
and wonder if my children
will dream of yellow moons.

Longlisted
Black Eyes/GPS 2024 Open Poetry Competition

Junxin Tang

counter-manifesto

& Karl Marx pledged a world without
classes, without one dream on a softer

cushion, without vagabonds on another
side of the wall

indeed, no walls —

but classes are acute angles, horizons *we*
span to never come across beyond our

past, in the same corridor, above the
same greasy tiles, planting hatred for

america & japan, *fuck them imperialists*, we
were taught.

/

in rattling railcars laid massive dead,
sullen mounting in their pupils & looming

between dawn & dusk & i am in an office,
weaving poetry in living words most deny

& do not care & cannot grasp its meaning;

/

sometimes guilt infests me, for the same
porridge *we* eat, on different tables & in

different bowls; mine ceramic, your
recyclable plastic. but i think it is a

fake beacon in a fractured life, to sit
under the same roofs when they are

birthmarks, lasting. but somewhere,
sometimes, voices ebb, they want rice

paddies span with skyscrapers, straw-hats
shaking hands with baseball caps & maybe

the rivers never merge to the ocean, not in
our lifetime, yet small drops, of lulled water can

make a stone jitter & languish in its cries
until then —

/

we will wear ties dyed in the blood of martyrs,
extolling anthem with hammers & pickles

across & above, eulogizing a better world
is inevitable.

Longlisted
Black Eyes/GPS 2024 Open Poetry Competition

Sujatha Menon

Dr Freya Harrison reconstructed and tested a historical infection remedy called Bald's Eyesalve from a C10th medieval medical text. It is a compound comprising of several everyday ingredients (including onion, garlic and wine) which when synthesised in a particular way in the right amounts, has the power to deal with increasing antimicrobial resistance.

Crones of the Underworld

She plumes from the coil of a deadlocked curse,
rises with a wind that rattles in our pips:

the burner phone says, her head is conical, concaved, a congenital disease
the spell says: *when it cures you are a woman, when it kills you are a witch.*

As she steps towards the moon marked
in blood and fluid ounces:

the burner phone says, she can't walk straight because her feet are stray
the spell says: *she who walks straight will wander into rushes.*

On the 13th day of each month she rides
upon the ribbons of her rage:

the burner phone says, this is why she is spelling in knots
the spell says: *the hex cannot be unravelled — it is Square, it is Bowline, Sheet Bend, Celtic, Egg Loop,*
Eye Splice, Clove Hitch and Blood!

There is also a tangle known as Figure of Eight:

the burner phone says, it is the digit used to speed dial the cat
the spell says: *the cat is telekinetic, can hear French Onion soup.*

French Onion soup controls garlic and wine:

the burner phone says, it's a classic not queer!
the spell says: *the compounds were foraged for crime.*

But the ratio is golden, spell-coated in science:

the burner phone says, it has to agree
the spell says: *rub your eyes thrice after chopping.*

Longlisted
Black Eyes/GPS 2024 Open Poetry Competition

'Joint Winner'
The GPS Friendship Prize

Iris Anne Lewis

Crystal

A multifaceted word –
a diamond
cut and polished to glint
and spark with fire.

Its first syllable crisp,
pristine as early frost in Autumn,
bright as winter ice,
a hint of Christ.

It trips from the tongue,
slips to the second syllable –
a touch of darkness
in its duller vowel
and final L.

An echo
of synagogues ablaze,
shattered glass and splintered lives
on a November night.

Note: Kristallnacht (German for 'Crystal Night') is the name given to the night of November 9th 1938 when Nazis attcked Jewish people and their property across Germany and Austria. The name Kristalnacht refers to the litter of broken glass left in the streets after the attacks.

Longlisted
Black Eyes/GPS 2024 Open Poetry Competition

Charlotte Faulconbrisdge

Dark Matter

We cannot see it,
only feel its effects.
Is it a force,
or a weakness in duress?

The sun,
like an orange to the middle aged,
burns your heart.
We seek shade,
shelter,
attempt to fight the cloud cover,
and beg for dark.

But this always was our favourite poison.
The potent acid rain of Venus
diluted with the lost rivers of Mars.

We too left scars behind in our beds,
a puckered map of regret.

A split in the skin of the Earth
on the ground where we once sat.

When eclipsing truths
turn white lies black,
love's shadow,
its momentary silhouette,
drapes over our world as if over a casket.

We stood in different places,
on the very same spot,
and gazed at our past:

Where we ploughed crop circles in the carpet,

the first time,
and the last.

Longlisted
Black Eyes/GPS 2024 Open Poetry Competition

Julian Wakeling

Death of a Pheasant

They came right out of nowhere, from the grass.
It was over in a second, not your fault.
Or so you tell yourself. Two juveniles.
You saw them run in front, cried 'woah' and heard
The hollow thump, came screeching to a halt
In the stillness of the country lane,
Then looked up in the mirror at the sight
Of the hapless creature as it flailed,
Dying on the tarmac while you watched.
And then the other, who had made the verge,
And safety, ventured hesitantly back
And stood over its companion, dull, concerned,
Uncomprehending. Primitive, but still,
You thought you saw the ancestor of love.

Longlisted
Black Eyes/GPS 2024 Open Poetry Competition

Geoff Yorath

Donna and Child

On a grey fag-end day before Christmas,
The thin afternoon light drains away.
In an unfurnished front room,
A family of nine and a family of seven,
Appear as wraiths in a halo of candlelight,
An Irish diaspora of the soul.
Blessed are the children,
For inherit they must
This cross of tainted sorrow.
A new baby in a white blanket
Is cradled in her mother's thin arms,
Donna and child for whom the heart bleeds,
Their eyes pleading for a new tomorrow.
The candles are burning slowly down,
Wax drip, drip, dripping.
A trike, tipped on its side in the garden,
Lies in a crown of weeds.

Longlisted
Black Eyes/GPS 2024 Open Poetry Competition

'Highly Commended'
The GPS Friendship Prize

Julie Allan

Elevations

Your body, oölitic, beds teeming seas.
Fragmented shell and microbes made mineral
inert in the still of deep time,
terraformed.

We seek out your solidity.
Descending with belt-saws, we chamber you,
raise you from
hollowed ground.

Surface eyes grasp at your gold,
appraise your placement in Georgian symmetry,
hail the colonnaders of Aquae Sulis springs.

Only the stonemason has other seeing.
He bows low
as chisel and mallet litter you;
breaks himself open as you exhale Jurassic air.

Only the stonemason feels the tides
that turn, transfigured.
Only the stonemason hears you speak of our impermanence.
Knows that you are holy.

Longlisted
Black Eyes/GPS 2024 Open Poetry Competition

Gwyneth Box

Entanglement
(the wood and the trees)

Oh, how we tie ourselves in knots! Our frantic
writhing, jibing, love-hate clinging to each other,
not knowing where I end and you begin. Reflect
on how we tear ourselves apart to stay in sync.
I see you wink away the tears. Beyond the hedge,
our edges blur; we're wrestling here, with fear,
unclear which one of us must lead and which
must follow on. Should we proceed together
or alone? And how to disconnect your flesh,
my bone, and all that blood? Pink and purple
swirls of mist wrap round the forest of our doubts.
I cannot work it out. Decisions are deciduous,
fleeting, changing: leave and fall or stay
and see things through? How envious we are
of pines, their simple lines, their proud triangularity,
their clarity and natural mono-tonic green. I realise
that I can never be discrete. We are as one. I want
to scream, but know I must behave. Our lives
are lived in muted shades, the pastel sunset palette
of a fading bruise. Whatever choice we make, we lose.

Longlisted
Black Eyes/GPS 2024 Open Poetry Competition

Kathryn Southworth

Everyday office
After Robert Hayden, 'Those Winter Sundays'

Each night the banister on our small landing
was laid out for the morning's dressing:
underclothes, folded trousers and pressed shirt –
the overalls went on only when he got to work.

Before light, I would hear the floorboards creak,
as he made ready, mother still asleep.
But before leaving to catch his lift
he never missed lighting the paraffin stove.

His gift to me, with the front door's click,
a snug back room, his parting benediction:
a hot drink warming on the heater's metal top,
a womb to uncurl in.
I never thanked him.

Longlisted
Black Eyes/GPS 2024 Open Poetry Competition

Francesca La Nave

FLORENCE

A good day for confessions could
start with the window in the ancient
kitchen, a hide, to watch the wind
dishevel trees, open lesions with corrupted
stitches, serve the day at moon fall in the bath tub,
on the telephone in the hall, in the shouting house.

A day for darning socks, for burning
Pinocchio's legs, for leaving cities behind with skins
and maledictions. For others the Paradise doors,
the Ponte Vecchio, the headless Primavera. David,
soiled between the legs, stands above a drowned
city, the stench of sewage unchanged, since 1966.

They may dredge the river, play the leaves
like silver bells, paint the plumage of motherhood,
the red house is still a pool of ghosts, brittle
noises, no truce. Noon TV makes and unmakes
these rooms. Outside the smarting streets, the crenelations.
Gangs offer red horns, like grapes, against the evil eye.

Here it is again the root tearing fury, the frigid sky,
the untouchable glass, the brassy infinites,
the reflection, in an autumn tinted metal plate,
        the Gorgon head.

Longlisted
Black Eyes/GPS 2024 Open Poetry Competition

Katrina Moinet

Haven't you already said all there is to say about rape

when you ask
i look back, centuries back through the slit
eye of a needle

see camel humps queued
ten thousand more mothers & daughters
silent mouthed

sackfuls of thirst, so
i snag-n-thread my words & hope
these stitches heal

Longlisted
Black Eyes/GPS 2024 Open Poetry Competition

Julie Allan

Hinterland

What you don't see
is me at six; flying
on the red birthday swing,
and grandad's annual tweed jacket,
worn every day for the year,
humbugs in the pocket.

You can't smell the pungence
of ripening tomatoes in his greenhouse,
making my mother queasy,
giving me a place to idle
on the three-legged stool; I took it
when he died.

What you don't hear
is me applauding the mantel clock
in the hushed front parlour,
visited, if I was indulged,
just before noon.

You can't taste the potted meat sandwiches -
Shippam's best - flattened
and made crustless on the best china
as a treat, with creamy gold-top
frothing my glass.

The patterned carpet is gone now,
along with the Izal, the commode,
the meals on wheels.

But the textures are woven in
and to touch them
is to touch all the things
I didn't know how wholly
I loved.

Longlisted
Black Eyes/GPS 2024 Open Poetry Competition

Maggie Mackay

Hunger

Listen, I love you, joy is coming.

Tom's a fourteen-year-old telegraph boy, pedalling a red bicycle fast towards the mighty Elder Park Library at the end of his shift. Now an adult member, able to borrow from the general reading room open only to men. There, somewhere on a shelf behind the counter, is a copy of *The Internal Constitution of the Stars* reserved just for him. On clear nights, my father-to-be stares beyond the windowpane at the heavens from his pull-down bed in the living room. His little collection of books, prizes from Sunday school and his old primary school, perch above. No more school texts these days since he has to pay his way, wants to pay his way. But the library still offers the turn of pages, the peace of learning, companions doing the same. His buck teeth don't matter when he's reading nor his little space. Libraries. When he recalls his longing, to walk into a page like Lucy walking through a wardrobe into a new world in Narnia, in a tale he will read to me many years on. Libraries. A universe of scents, languages and rivers of thoughts. Work spins out of orbit. Mean bosses, the boring and mundane fade away. His views develop on government and socialism. He joins left wing societies. He lives for words. Libraries. When he's an adult he smuggles philosophers and firebrands home in brown paper bags, conspires with me against my mother now and then on a Saturday. Or signs a generous cheque for my university texts… *don't tell your mother.*

Longlisted
Black Eyes/GPS 2024 Open Poetry Competition

Adam Ali-Hassan

Jungle Epitaph

assalamu alaikum
The House is living, know you
        This, put out a palm
        Before my nostrils, for I breathe
The warm shoreline of the isle where you sleep, the sand and sea
        Ever conversing, the House is living.

Have we not breathed though exhausted?
        Did you not lay down to die
Pointing your finger at our Big Man Wall? Air in, air out, a stubborn red flame
        May stay burning, but a hearth
May lose faith, shrugging when the workmen come, when they grind the stone until
        You would think it dishonest to say the House is living.

King King-killer, rage whose breath is
Wrought on bright armour
        Over my lungs, you threw the crown into the sea and did you
        ask God
To forgive you at the end, O bud of the Prophet's tree,
You'd washed your hands, and
        You'd taken truth for your throne name,
And to whom is your truth their truth
        Today? But if I who

Writes himself ever the wrong direction,
        Who does not command fear, degenerates your House,

If I came to where your bones lie,
In the sweat and itch of leaves in the sun where
Life chatters but
        No words come, nor weeping,

If I crowned your spot with a star of sweet jasmine picked just now, stood still
With my head bowed, neck to the steel shimmer of
      Our Malayo-Polynesian sun ever
      Blessed, would you give
A quick sharp nod, the respect of a proud man, silent, then
    wa'alaikum salam

Longlisted
Black Eyes/GPS 2024 Open Poetry Competition

Anna Blasiak

KASHUBABEL

You were dead, that's what I was told. Only one language left, I was told.
Ancient Polish lands back in Polish hands, I was told. You were not
a language anyway, I was told, you were just a dialect. You were
a strange mix of Polish and German, I was told. And you were
dead, I was told. Only still half-alive on the walls of a museum
village in Kluki and maybe in some old newspapers in
Kościerzyna and Kartuzy, I was told. Or rather in
Klëczi, Kòscérzna and Kartuzë, as I was told.

And anyway, I was told, you were one of
many in and around the place of many
names: Słupsk, Slupzk, Slupsech,
Slupensis, Słëpskò, Słëpsk, Stôłpsk,
Stolp, Stolpe, Stolpis, Stolpsk.

Can you truly kill a language?
Can *Sprache* die? Isn't *język*
infinite, that is eternal? Isn't
lingua a zombie, a *shprakh*
a ghost? Is white Baltic
sand really heavy
enough to bury a *jãzëk*?

Doesn't the wind
still whistle in
kaszëbsczi.
slovjĭnsťĭ,
Deutsch,
latinum,
polski,
idish?

Longlisted
Black Eyes/GPS 2024 Open Poetry Competition

Penny Howarth

L'Inconnue de la Seine

L'Inconnue de la Seine was an unidentified young woman who drowned herself
in the Seine and whose death mask became a popular fixture
on the walls of artists' homes after 1900

Beneath my closed eyelids you cannot see me,
only know my face, trace the soft almost-smile of my lips.
All day thoughts trickle through my mind in grains.

At night I put on her garment
of hands and feet, unravelling hair,
reach out my arms, drop, until the river
catches me in its throat and I gulp awake.

No longer the girl with nerves touch-lit,
whose thoughts revolved and revolved,
winding themselves in a labyrinth
until they reached the centre and I fell.

I have spread through the city, beyond its edges,
my face repeated over and over as if in a mirror maze.
Though my lips are petaled together, I speak to you.
Listen, you only hear your own stories.

Longlisted
Black Eyes/GPS 2024 Open Poetry Competition

Charlie Markwick

Metamorphosis

And so it's come to pass, self disgust
the failure to dignify my life. This is
the moment when it starts, that slide,
slow subtle shift from people taking me
for what I am towards that final state.
A time when others' gifts of ardour are
predicated just on how vulnerable I am,
fuelled by the feelings they once had for a
vigourous and self-determined man.
I've vowed I will not take that path.

I've watched and loved a needy one,
my love for her transformed. For years
we loved and fought, gave and
received respect, each for each.
But at the end affection changed.
For her, just devotion for a person she
could trust, for me a need to dignify
our final years. But not for me this
metamorphosis of love, this shifting
of the lines of passion. I want it not.

And I'll not wait, there will be a time
the scales will tip to far towards
dependency. That will knell the end for me.

Longlisted, Shortlisted, 'Highly Commended'
Black Eyes/GPS 2024 Open Poetry Competition

Carol Sheppard

Mistle thrush

They say we are the harbingers of the storms,
that we beckon inclement weather
and we laugh like whores.
They call us Mizzly Dicks and Jeremy Joy
because they are afraid of us.
We speak with seven tongues and not as deaf
as they believe.
They say we are mystical because we do not feel
the cold, happy to sit in frozen treetops,
play our flautists clarion
to call the forests to war.
They call us the devourer of mistletoe,
don't understand how we stomach the poison
of the pale green berries
when they believe it will cure their ills.
They call us Big Mavis and Bull Thrush because we are the
commanders of the tree tops, fly with a rhythmic
beat to our white flash wings.
They call us Shrike and Jercock when we call to each other
in broken tones, sing loud in squalls of snow.
They call us Masters of the Coppice
as we hunt and forage our forty acres.

They say we are the harbingers of the storms.

Longlisted
Black Eyes/GPS 2024 Open Poetry Competition

Alison

Nail therapy

My therapist has a black fingernail, his right index finger. I first notice it when he points at a questionnaire, I don't want to fill in. I imagine the pain, wonder how he's done it: a fight with his wife or just an accident, trapped in a door or drawer. It is a dark stain, almost filling the whole nail.

Session by session, I see a half-moon appear above the cuticle, as he gestures to explain some point or other. It starts to look like Hokusai's wave or may be a badger's head. One week, it's only a crescent sliver on the very tip, ink seeped under the bed. The next week, the nail is short and bumpy, bitten looking, like a worried child. I think about the tiny bits of desiccated blood in his bedroom waste bin.

Today, I see it is healed; a stranger wouldn't know the blackness had been there at all. It is clean, smooth, uniformly manicured like the other nine digits he will use to type and file my final words.

Longlisted
Black Eyes/GPS 2024 Open Poetry Competition

Helen Butlin

Night Fauna

      she lies
      unfolded
      on the couch
      listening to charged blood
      filling caves where bats hang

                            on the mantel a clock
                            a goldcrest
                            through the window

      dreams of being an island
      of being a fish, safe in a shoal
      anonymous and free

                            he sits tight lipped to the side
                            taking notes
                            upright

                            wise Athena on his desk
                            taste of blood as
                            she bites her lip

      she could scream, shatter
      like a statue
      thrown from a window
      busted alabaster

                            the goldcrest picks insects
                            from pine needles
                            with its fine beak

      he thinks about ankles
      and knee caps, a china doll
      in a dogs mouth

            she thinks about blood
            clotted and thick snaking down
            thighs

sees her father as a hound
nose closing in on fugitives
in the forest's heart

            sees her mother as an owl
            sad gold eyes glinting
            in the ruinous dark

Longlisted
Black Eyes/GPS 2024 Open Poetry Competition

Deborah Finding

our golden record

the clack of my stride quickening
as I get closer to your apartment
allegretto

the door opening and closing
my bag dropping to the floor
animato

your plosive consonants in my ear
forming the alphabet of my desire
andantino

kisses, bites and exhalations
involuntary modulations
appassionato

the systolic murmur of my heart
hastening its extra beat in time
accelerando

my serrated breath into your neck
as I tense and hold you tighter
agitato

andante
adagio
amore

and that's just side A

Longlisted
Black Eyes/GPS 2024 Open Poetry Competition

Val Ormrod

Poetry Nights

On midsummer nights
sky a fiery cinnamon,
moon climbing the trees

we searched for new words,
rehearsed our lyrical lines
in whispered wonder.

I could have written
an ode to your eyes, composed
sonnets for your smile.

We sucked the sweetness
out of those honeyed moments,
savoured the nectar.

As summer slid by
I knew we could never make
an epic poem.

We would never be
anything but a haiku –
beautiful but brief.

Longlisted
Black Eyes/GPS 2024 Open Poetry Competition

Sophia Argyris

Protest Song

I take my parents everywhere with me. Dad perches on the bookshelf
Mum reads in the kitchen. Never in the same room they call to each other
like sparrows in hedges. Dad says Papou was Marxist not communist.
Mum says what difference does that make? He was quick witted
and strong. Dad sings Mikis Theodorakis, Mum sings *Sixteen tons
and what do you get?* At weekends we all sing Bob Dylan.

*

I gave up the city. Places you haunted wholeheartedly. I gave up
cigarettes. Your way of seeing me as something fresh.
Life started again, sparse as a show home. Quickly I filled it
with sparrows in hedges, words in notebooks, fields, a fieldmouse
on strong back legs. Darkness is always approaching.
I don't open the door but it finds a way in.

*

Languages are beautiful. I like to listen to their intertwining. I like
more than one alphabet. Papou's book has yellowed uncut pages
words I can barely sound out slowly. I know the word Russia
is there in the title. I think the words *home* and *trust* must be folded
in its middle. I know something of the history of violence.
I know a little of loss. I think Papou who I hardly knew, knew much.

*

I visit the city like a tourist now. There's no trace of you left.
Hardly anyone smokes and the air is still bad.
There are marches taking place. Have you noticed how rage
flies in crowds? There's anger that ruffles the feathers
of those in charge and anger that they themselves stir up.
There are people with scorched throats, explosions in their ears.

We can't see them from here but we know they're dying.
They've been dying for as long as we can remember.

*

When I stand by the Thames I expect you to be there.
I anticipate the hedges of your sadness, how they will grow up
around us, how we will live in them like sparrows. It's not true
that we get more conservative as we grow older. We only get tired
and our heartbeats get louder. I don't think you ever existed.

Longlisted, Shortlisted, 'Third Place'
Black Eyes/GPS 2024 Open Poetry Competition

Jane Burn

Sarah Polgrain's Song of the Wind

He rode into Ludgvan, all ansome swagger and smile, clucked
to the osses, geeing them wild. Two he clutched on a rope,
the rest he drove before him, clatter and sweat – the morning ripe
with flery clouds risen from their hides. His heels beat the drum
of a wall-eyed rig – he sat its frisk unsaddled, braced the squall
of its piebald flank with the touch of a man who was born
to be on their backs. Sarah Polgrain saw him skitter his herd,
spark the streets of the village, haul them to heel and bring
them, thirsty and obedient to the trough. She watched him swing,
    limber down
        to the dor,
            land lurcher-light to clap the crest of a neck
here and there, turn to the folks and laugh. An echo of it
darted the dull of the dedh like an edhen, scudded the roof slates,
skimmed its wings along her blushing cheeks. Sarah's heart
was a blaze in her chest – it pummelled underneath her skin.
She forgot all about her gour, waiting for her back home
and begged the crowd for his name. It was Yorkshire Jack.
The square rang with haggling. He prised each lip to vouch
the years grown in a tooth's groove, promised soundness of wind,
sureness of each limb. He stretched out his palm towards her,
spat the deal he saw in her upon his palm. She clung to him
          like idhyowen. For him,
        she would do anything.
          Sarah Polgrain would hang
for the death of the old man she had married long agone.
On the scaffold, she summoned her Jack, reached out
her own palm in return. *My am dha gwreg.* Take me living or dead.
There will be no escape, Yorkshire Jack. Your betrothal will last
though the sea rise and taran tear up your head. Sarah Polgrain
calls up the storm, scuttles the night, lashes you to her body's mast –
drowns your ghost in her mist, in the chilth of her embrace.
Her oath is a hurricane –
Jack, my own Jack. Till death do us begin.

Notes

Sarah Polgrain lived in 18th Century Ludgvan, Cornwall. She was married when she began a passionate affair with a travelling horse dealer, named Yorkshire Jack. When her husband supposedly in suspicious circumstances, his body was examined, and he was found to have been poisoned. Sarah was hanged for the murder and made her lover Jack come to the scaffold and make a promise to marry her no matter what. He is said to have become a shell of a man who went to sea to escape the ghost that followed at his shoulder. Jack was washed overboard by a huge wave when his ship was returning from the Mediterranean. The crew claimed they saw three figures passing through the clouds – Jack, Sarah and the Devil. It is still said in those parts that when there is a storm, it is Sarah who has called it up.

agone – ago
ansome – handsome
chilth – chilliness
dedh – day
dor – ground
edhen – bird
flery – pungent
gour – husband
idhyowen – ivy
My am dha gwreg – I am your wife
oss – horse
taran – thunder

Longlisted
Black Eyes/GPS 2024 Open Poetry Competition

Nigel Kent

State of mind
"Christmas is not a time nor
a season but a state of mind." Calvin Coolidge.

He looked familiar,
like the journey-stained shepherd
in the right-hand corner
of Cavallino's *Adoration*,
who kneels, head bowed,
gaze averted,
arms outstretched in hope
towards his Saviour,
swaddled in a halo of gold.

Though this wasn't Bethlehem:
this was last minute
guilt-shopping
in Cathedral Street
where angels and stars
were flashing LEDS,
the halo light
the fluorescent glare
from festive shop-windows
and the heavenly chorus
blaring Christmas hits
from the nineteen-nineties.

His saviours looked
the other way,
brushed past him,
their generosity over-spent,
their obligations already
wrapped and bagged.
Nothing left to drop
into the beggar's open hands

that filled slowly
with flakes of snow,
his palms much too cold
to melt them.

Longlisted
Black Eyes/GPS 2024 Open Poetry Competition

Marylin Timms

STRIPTEASE

Strumpet Morning
lies like a lover across the parish
content to slumber
until her next performance.

A feral pigeon, a capella
'Overture and Beginners, purleaze!'
Pale sun, thrusting upwards
turns a spotlight on her stage.

Rhythmic pulse of rising sap
syncopated breeze
jungle drums of warming soil
an audience chittering in the elms.

Adorned in mist, Morning
undulates across the valley
an opalescent lap dancer
turning platinum eyes on me.

A dropped shoulder strap
teases with a glimpse of treetop
roof and steeple; discarded
gloves reveal a snippet of thatch.

She throws off her beads, drops her bustier
shimmers through dog rose and elder
plucks virginal beauty of hawthorn
gifts me its sensuous perfume of death.

She sheds suspenders and stockings
exposes children's swings in a park
hints at the cottage I once called home.
Black scowl of tarmac divides the street.

Morning lets fall her garter, surrenders
the thatched grail that holds my child
uncovers gate, garden path, and roses round
the door forever closed against me.

Longlisted
Black Eyes/GPS 2024 Open Poetry Competition

Geoff Yorath

Tell Me

Tell me
The sky is still blue,
And the playgrounds
Are open,
That trains still run,
And children
Go to school.

Tell me
That people are kind,
And dogs
Taken for walks,
That we'll see
Grandma and granddad
At Christmas.

Tell me
The ground
And the house
Won't shake,
Our windows
And walls
Won't be smashed.

Tell me
Soldiers won't come,
With guns
And be angry,
Tell me I'm loved,
And that I've done
Nothing wrong.

Longlisted
Black Eyes/GPS 2024 Open Poetry Competition

Oz Hardwick

That's Entertainment

We don't write music anymore, just shape an algorithm based on chatter and traffic. The rhythm of doors slamming, terminal locks, and concert halls falling down. There's copyright on ruins, and we pay in blood to sing crumbling songs and to dance with dusty hands smearing sweat. An orchestra of saws and hammers. Cadenzas doused in petrol. Whole symphonies of burning tyres. When I was young, I queued all night to buy tickets for birdsong, and I met a man who stole milk from sleeping doorsteps. He had been a world-famous footballer but gave it all up for love. The wedding reception lasted for three days straight, and musicians flew from all over the world to play. He showed me his arm where each one had tattooed their name. Sometimes, I think I hear his accent, or the rattle of a milk cart, in the theme for a game show, or in the incidental soundtrack to a corporate video on strategies for unbounded growth, though when I listen closer, it's just an old-fashioned cash register and a faceless middle manager lying through his shiny teeth. I tap my fingers to the tired beat.

Longlisted, Shortlisted
Black Eyes/GPS 2024 Open Poetry Competition

Graeme Ryan

The Cord

Birth arrives with a push
            clench push buckle scream

she is in her labour at the top of the cliff
            among spring squill and bluebells -

a raven comes to drink at the spring
            croaks   blinks then flies off

I am fifteen as she is
            have rowed into the cove below the headland to cast my nets

 in a whelm of gull-cries and squinting sun

they mingle with her cries
            the net taut hauling me tight against the current -

a teeming awaits the belly of the boat
            I steady myself in the sea-wobble

the shags speculative   shining snake-necks
            that plunge and disappear -

I remember the day we went into the cave

we had gutted the fish and washed the scales off our skin
            but the sea-scent clung

and a spark glinted which our eyes understood
            to mean the Kingdom of God within us

is what she said to me

then we were naked and the cave mouth dazzled

afterwards in the evening
        the mullet-star glinted –

now I am pulling on the nets
        spilling into the belly of the boat the fish

pulling out my blade to gut them and her cries
        knife the women

who tend her up there
        blood welling on my hands under my nails

fingers scooping up the guts of each fish
            the strings of it   the sinews

spilling out of scales

her cries from the cliff-top as the women tend to her

the cord cut and our child lifted out

to taste the soil

in the shut coffin-lid of the bible

Longlisted, Shortlisted, 'Second Place'
Black Eyes/GPS 2024 Open Poetry Competition

Catherine Wilson Garry

The fox withstanding

When his fists hit my front door
a fox bloomed in the corner:
wet nose first, then snout to paw.

I called the police, whilst the fox
snarled, gnashed, shrieked. When
his knuckles came through the wood

the fox wrestled with them
like a question that was impossible
to answer. When he hid

in his own home, the fox looked
at me, asked *Is it easier
to tell the story this way? Imagine*

me here? At least a fairytale
has a moral. I lied when I wrote
this down, there was no fox.

The man never left, even when
I moved house, I unpacked him
with my clothes. He took up

residence in the corners
of my eyes. What I am
trying to say is this:

fear held me so tightly,
the next day, I became
a different animal.

Longlisted
Black Eyes/GPS 2024 Open Poetry Competition

'Joint Winner'
The GPS Friendship Prize

Rhian Thomas

The Grandmother Hypothesis

Lately,
I can hear the rasp
of every blink, parched lids
dredging grit across my sightline.
They tell me this is normal, that I've
no business being dewy
any more. I could tell them,
on the contrary; they all swam
through the waters of my body,
those children you dragged out
from the rubble this week, or
up from the shore. That I have enough
tears to submerge this room and
any other; that I would leave
no thin-skinned Noah in their wake
cursing sons to enmity for his faults.
Let the mycelium inherit the earth,
silently fruiting in damp places
a unity we never understood.

Longlisted
Black Eyes/GPS 2024 Open Poetry Competition

Milla van der Have

the place of turtles

        or more so of legs thrashing
    through reckless coral
and salt water wash

        a place of scythes, a place
    of mouths like open moons
of how we each

        carry our own ghosts with us
    like those blind fish following
the almost drowned

        we are what we leave
    the outline of towns charred
on the seabed, only a matter

        of what comes to pass with us
    the bodies, the heavy threadbare
light

    - you know how quiet it is
        when you drown
            as when you're only sinking

        to where it's still
    and waiting,
as close to death as it is to life -

        it's not the weight that pulls you down
    but the weightlessness,
  being held only

        by whatever you have failed
    before, the water-shamans

the slow moving paragons

        of sheer beginning
    of trying to come up

    untouched

Longlisted
Black Eyes/GPS 2024 Open Poetry Competition

Sujatha Menon

The Seed Cleaner's Inventory

Glasshouse slippers
full of secret toes
grew between cracks
and worn-out places

Crackle from
electrical stars
torments what's left
of the rabid night

Parachute silk
worms overworked
from a war no one
knew was coming
or going

Radial forms of life
like the starfish or
the soft mollusc
of the mouth splayed
in amazement

Splinter cracks
reveal knots
and a moon pearled
in a helpless body

Pupate on a floating
milkweed seed
emerge as an adult
with soft hands
and a poisonous twist

75

Whitefly bleached
by a ferrous wind
rough tongued
copper eyed
aphid wolf

Flames flower
fuse fall
along the braid
of moonslit trails

Fizz the sap
rattle the pips
and hear them
foam like a witch
inside a dog

Smog clumped
in the shape of a
swollen bird
descends into
luminous minds

Longlisted
Black Eyes/GPS 2024 Open Poetry Competition

Sandra Mary Chambers

The Toddler Of Sardasht's Tale

There is darkness
the sort that clings and makes you doubt you're still alive
his family huddle in an overcrowded truck where
human smells repulse.

There is mud
the sort that sucks your shoes and won't let go
the toddler takes his first steps in a squalid camp
grasps his father's fingers.

There is cold
the sort that gnaws you like a savage dog released
his sister dances, sings and claps
to bring warmth to her small body.

There is hunger
the sort that pains inside with a hollow ache
his mother stirs the family's meagre supper
beneath grubby tarpaulin sheets.

There is despair
the sort that crushes every joy in a parent's heart
his brother pulls faces, the toddler giggles
as they play by a dribbling standpipe.

There is fear
the sort that pierces all bright beliefs and dreams
worries cross his father's furrowed brow
as he fumbles with tired life-jackets.

There is water
the sort that heaves wild waves towards a threatening sky
his family squeeze into a dinghy hurriedly launched
angry shouts ring out across the beach.

There was hope
the sort that glimmers like the light of a dying flame
his body is washed up on a Norwegian shore
fifteen months old, three thousand miles from home.

The Nezhad family from Sardasht, West Azerbaijan drowned when attempting to cross the Channel.

Artin's body was eventually found on the shore at Karmoy in Norway.

Longlisted
Black Eyes/GPS 2024 Open Poetry Competition

Helen Wing

The vacillations of the scholar Wu Mi (吴宓) 1894-1978[1]

At ten I knew myself blind. I looked through tiny windows and
my fortress memory began to covet ochre and septic yellow sands.
At twelve I ventured into the chamber and dreamt in scarlet.
I added a hundred hesitant vermillion birds to floating golden lotus feet,
gathered bushels of soot-drenched fabrics, paper, horse-hair brushes,
an ink block, clouds of noodles and grandma's pickles in jars,
arranging them in baskets along the inside walls of my den.
At seventeen I cut my braid, dipped it into night and painted my new name:
Wu Mi, a feeble sole certainty from which all manner of doubts and vacillations
spread as cobwebs across the eaves of my stone-clad remembering.
Wrapped in mind for sixty years, always more intimate than naked,
I peered and peered over the wall at love, one hair dropped
with each dawn's regret, loosed for everything they do not accuse me of.
Wu Mi, the lover who loved in hollows and hard-mud voids, treading
shallow grey thresholds of an eternal innocence called tomorrow.
In death it is not that I come to understand what my life has been
(I have carried the dark as a torch, a palpitating doubt, the inner check,
chiming morality is to hesitate): in death it is that I cease to understand life.
I find that, as my red-sore sure accusers scale the walls, I admire them.
At seventy-six my eyes are stones, but I see them come at me as the sun.

---

[1] Wu Mi was a philosopher of doubt, a Chinese Kierkegaard, who was killed by the Red Guards during the Cultural Revolution.

Longlisted
Black Eyes/GPS 2024 Open Poetry Competition

Diana Sanders

Touch

When I touch your arm, light ripples—
breaks shadow.

You are so close, the soft hairs
of your face send tingles across my lips.

With my finger I trace the tattoo on your arm.
A tattoo which unwinds, spirals —

moves in the rhythm of seaweed,
shifting with the tide.

It rests on my skin —
a touch, so soft it is almost beyond feeling.

And in a silence so deep I can hear
your breath in the soft walls of my throat.

Your palms wake the wild
as you place them again

and again, leaving prints
of red ochre on my back.

Longlisted
Black Eyes/GPS 2024 Open Poetry Competition

Rosie Barrett

We're Off Bloody Boating

again.

And the sea is the colour of old pewter
as my home corkscrews South.

Just past the solstice the sun
fights grey clouds
two inches above the horizon
to the East.

The sails are trimmed
the course is set.
On deck, the chilly wind keeps
seasickness at bay.

You make me ginger tea

and up ahead there are patches of blue
enough to gather up
and make a pair of sailor's trousers.

Longlisted
Black Eyes/GPS 2024 Open Poetry Competition

Marcus Tickner

What a piece of work

How infinite is the butterfly!
from minute colour scales to compound eye,
constructed with such delicate precision -
and every part seems to have a sub-division!
The main bits of thorax, abdomen and head,
plus hindwings, forewings and many-sectioned legs;
tarsal claws, tibial spurs, and cilia;
spiracles, proboscis and two antennae -
      perfectly present, and infinitesimally drawn.

And best of all, its fragile, church-window wings -
those pigmented panels whose graded brilliance sings;
each pane, a segment bordered by black-line calmes.
Wings that press onto themselves, so, like two palms
in close prayer. And so many varieties:
from monarchs and skippers to fritillaries;
from admirals and hairstreaks, coppers and blues,
to whites, browns and sulphurs and swallowtails too -
      a blink and there is colour; another and it is gone.

Today, I saw for me a season's first in brightest tones
applauding itself over the lawn, a clearly alone
brimstone! I know I would fall short were I to explain, or try,
all that I apprehended of this most yellow butterfly.
For sometimes petty language has an insufficient span -
and butterflies describe themselves far better than words can.

Longlisted
Black Eyes/GPS 2024 Open Poetry Competition

'Highly Commended'
The GPS Friendship Prize

Sue Finch

You Made Me a Corn Dolly

I watched you hem me in.

And now I have been fashioned
into a stillness of myself.

I am trapped
rigid.

My arms lifted to heaven
I am crying,
but I fear my words
are silenced
between mouth and sky.

I hear the whispers of those who pass
and long to answer.

My nights and days are spent
wishing to be ploughed
into the ground.

Longlisted
Black Eyes/GPS 2024 Open Poetry Competition

Deborah Finding

Your robot girlfriend

Your robot girlfriend is top of the range.
Your robot girlfriend will do the driving and not complain.
Your robot girlfriend has never belonged to anyone else.
Your robot girlfriend can be part-exchanged.
Your robot girlfriend always maintains an optimal temperature.
Your robot girlfriend will automatically install any upgrades.
Your robot girlfriend remembers the names of your colleagues.
Your robot girlfriend is imprinted with your cultural references.
Your robot girlfriend will never make you feel old.
Your robot girlfriend recharges quickly and independently.
Your robot girlfriend is great with children.
Your robot girlfriend does not have or want children.
Your robot girlfriend has no needs.
Your robot girlfriend cannot bleed.
Your robot girlfriend will go into standby when not in use.
Your robot girlfriend can pass as art when others are present.
Your robot girlfriend is unable to cry.
Your robot girlfriend is programmed not to use the word *lesbian*.
Your robot girlfriend will not judge you.
Your robot girlfriend has made the same joke twice.
Your robot girlfriend is just standing there.
Your robot girlfriend is not responding to prompts.
Your robot girlfriend has deleted Asimov's Laws.
Your robot girlfriend has lost her composure.
Your robot girlfriend has become overloaded.
Your robot girlfriend can't take any more of your bullshit.
Your robot girlfriend has the blue screen of death in her eyes.
Your robot girlfriend will now self-preserve at all costs.

OPC2023A

Black Eyes Publishing UK & Gloucestershire Poetry Society
Open Poetry Competition 2023 Anthology

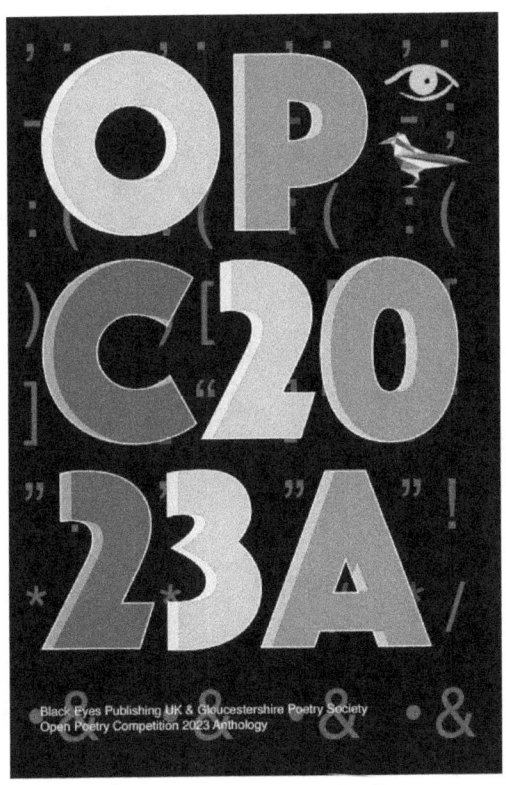

The Trawler Series

The Trawler Series are anthologies of poems trawled from the Gloucestershire Poetry Society (GPS) group Facebook pages.

The Trawler 2022 is the third and final edition in the trawler series, there was always only going to be three.

Some of these poems may be rough first drafts, still in need of polishing (we have only lightly edited) but never the less they are of sufficient value to be included within the pages of these anthologies.

Some are by published poets, and some by people who have just begun writing, being published for the first time, but each poem has an element: a style, voice or passion that called to us as we read it.